SCHOLASTIC

Fill-in-the-Blank Stories

PHONICS

50 Cloze-Format Practice Pages That Target and Teach Key Phonics Skills

by Linda B. Ross

New York • Toronto • London • Auckland • Sydney
Mexico City • New Delhi • Hong Kong • Buenos Aires

Teaching *Resources*

Editor: Joan Novelli
Cover design by Jason Robinson
Interior design by Holly Grundon
Cover and interior illustrations by Bari Weissman

ISBN-13: 978-0-439-45863-4
ISBN-10: 0-439-45863-3

1 2 3 4 5 6 7 8 9 10 40 15 14 13 12 11 10 09 08

Contents

Introduction

This book features 50 engaging cloze-format stories that provide the repeated practice children need to master essential phonics skills, including sound-spelling relationships and structural analysis. For each story, children use a word bank along with text and picture clues to fill in missing words. Each story offers opportunities for reading decodable words in context, letting young readers apply their growing knowledge of sound-spelling relationships and word parts to new words, while improving fluency and comprehension. A word search provides further practice in reading and spelling all target words.

What the Research Says

Phonics knowledge has a positive effect on a reader's ability to decode words and is a reliable predictor of later skill in reading comprehension. "Skilled readers recognize the majority of words they encounter in text quickly and accurately, independently of context." (Cunningham, 1975–76; Stanovich, 1984; as cited in *Phonics From A to Z* by Wiley Blevins; Scholastic, 2006)

What's Inside?

From a bird named Twinkle to a frog and a dog that are friends, the characters in these charming stories will bring children back again and again to build essential reading skills. Each student page follows a format that children will quickly learn to recognize, allowing them to focus their energies on using the words rather than figuring out what to do. Here's a look at the components for each page.

Phonics Skill: The heading at the top of each story page identifies the target phonics skill.

Fill-In Story: A cloze format invites children to fill in words to complete each story. Stories are carefully structured to meet the needs of early readers.

Word Bank: This list provides students with all the word choices they need to complete the story.

Illustration: An illustration accompanies each story, and supports early readers in understanding the text.

Word Search: This puzzle invites children to locate the target story words, reinforcing word recognition skills and building vocabulary.

Teaching With the Stories

Each story page focuses on one of the following areas: consonants and vowels (short and long), *r*-controlled vowels, variant vowels and diphthongs, consonant blends and digraphs, plurals, inflected endings, and contractions. You can use the stories in any order that best supports your goals for whole-class, small-group, and individual instruction. Model for children how to complete a page before having them do so on their own.

1. Display a story page so all children can see it (for example, by using an overhead).

2. Read the directions aloud, and then direct children's attention to the Word Bank. Point to each word in order as you read it. Think aloud about how words are similar—for example, pointing out those with the same vowel sound.

3. Direct children's attention to the title of the story. Read aloud the title, again noticing words that are similar in some way. You might take a moment to notice the illustration, and think aloud about what the story might be about.

4. As you read the story, model concepts of print, including where to begin, going from left to right, and the return sweep to the next line. Pause at each blank to think aloud about which word belongs in the blank. (It may be helpful for children to read on past a blank to finish a sentence, as the end of the sentence might provide clues to the missing word.) This is a good opportunity to teach strategies for figuring out the correct word choice, including through context. For example, in "Little Cub" (page 24), the last sentence reads "Get into the _____ and take a bath!" Point out that children can read past the blank to the word *bath*, and ask themselves, "Where do people take a bath? What word makes sense here?" This can help them recognize that *tub* is the word that best completes the sentence. Write in the word, and continue. (As another strategy, you might show children how to lightly draw a line through each word in the Word Bank as they use it.)

5. When you have filled in all of the blanks, read the story, modeling characteristics of fluency, such as using appropriate expression and pausing at punctuation.

6. Complete the Word Search, showing children how to look across, down, and diagonally—but not backward—for the words in the Word Bank. Place a check next to each word as you find it. Once you find all of the words, read them aloud.

Teaching Tip

After modeling how to use a story page, you might invite students to take turns at the overhead, modeling for you how to complete the same page (use a fresh copy). This will encourage independence as they complete story pages on their own.

Connections to the Language Arts Standards

T he story pages and extension activities in this book are designed to support you in meeting the following standards as outlined by Mid-continent Research for Education and Learning (McREL), an organization that collects and synthesizes national and state curriculum standards—and proposes what teachers should provide for their students to become proficient in language arts, among other curriculum areas.

Reading

○ Understands how print is organized and read

○ Uses mental images based on pictures and print to aid in comprehension of text

○ Uses meaning clues to aid comprehension and make predictions

○ Uses phonetic and structural analysis to decode unknown words

○ Understands level-appropriate sight words and vocabulary

○ Knows main ideas or theme, setting, main characters, main events, sequence, and problems in stories

○ Summarizes information found in texts (retells in own words)

○ Makes simple inferences regarding the order of events and possible outcomes

○ Relates stories to personal experiences

Source: *Content Knowledge: A Compendium of Standards and Benchmarks for K–12 Education* (4th ed.). Mid-continent Research for Education and Learning, 2004.

Classroom Management Tips

W hether you photocopy each story page at the time of use, or prepare class sets of the stories in advance, a simple storage system will make it easy to build a collection that you can keep on hand for later use or repeated practice.

○ Place each set of stories in a file folder. Tape or glue a sample page to the front for reference, or label the tab with the target phonics skill and title.

○ To encourage self-checking, create an answer key, filling in the words to each story and circling the words in the Word Search. Attach to the back of the envelope or file folder. Or, place answer keys in a binder. (For a complete set of answers, see pages 10–14.)

Teaching Tip

The activity pages in this book also support components of the Reading First program (U.S. Department of Education): phonemic awareness, phonics, vocabulary development, reading fluency, and reading comprehension strategies.

Activities to Use With Any Story

The activities here are designed to extend what students learn with the story pages. Use them to provide additional practice with phonics skills, to improve fluency and comprehension, and as springboards for students' own writing.

Word Wall Builders

Extend learning by creating word walls or charts based on target words from the stories.

1. Copy target words from a story on chart paper or a whiteboard.

2. Read the words with children and invite them to suggest other words that could go on the chart. Guide them to recognize the particular skill area and to match that in their suggestions. For example, for a word wall based on "A Bug on a Rug" (page 23) children can add new CVC words with the short *u* sound—for example, *fun*, *hug*, *run*, *bus*, *cup*, and *mud*.

3. Copy the words on large index cards or sheets of paper. Create pictures to go with as many words as possible (enlarge the illustration from the story page to illustrate words from the story, using an arrow to point out the corresponding area of the art). Display pictures and words as a word wall. Use removable adhesive to create a portable word wall that children can take to their desk and then return to the wall when finished.

4. Play word wall games to reinforce word recognition and spelling. For example, using a word wall based on "A Bug on a Rug," direct students' attention to the word *rug*. Then say, "I'm thinking of a word that rhymes with *rug*. What is it?" (*bug*) or "I see two words that begin with *h*. What are they?" (*hum*, *hug*)

Pocket Chart Practice

The short stories in this book lend themselves well to pocket chart activities. Suggestions for creating these activities follow.

Who Has the Word? Write each line of a story on a sentence strip, leaving spaces for the target words. Cut sentence strips to fit the spaces and write a target word on each. Distribute the word cards to different children. In the pocket chart, place sentence strips in order. Read aloud the story. When you come to a missing word ask, "Who has the word that goes here?" Have that child place the word in the correct space. Continue in this way to complete the story, and then read it aloud together.

Scrambled Stories: Write each sentence of a story on a sentence strip, filling in any missing words. Mix up the strips and place them in a pocket chart. Invite children to help you sequence the sentences to unscramble the story. Number the backs of the sentence strips so children can work independently or in pairs to place the sentences in order, and then check their work. As a variation, cut apart sentences into individual words. Challenge children to arrange the words in order.

Story Hunt

Use any story for an interactive experience that encourages children to take a closer look at the text.

1. Copy a story on chart paper, leaving spaces for the missing words. Copy the Word Bank to the side.

2. Have children help you fill in the missing words, and read the story together.

3. Then invite children to take turns hunting for something in the story, using a highlighter to mark it when they find it. Children can locate rhyming words, hunt for commas, or highlight words that name people, places, and things, as well as action words. The possibilities are endless. For example, in "Things I Like" (page 30), you might ask children to find the following:

- a word with a double *o* (*good*)
- a sentence that ends with "!" (and then discuss what this punctuation mark tells readers)
- a word that rhymes with *game* (*name*)
- a word that names something to eat (*pizza*)
- a word that ends with *th* (*with*)

Encouraging Comprehension

The stories in this book are short but provide many opportunities to practice comprehension strategies. After children complete a story, revisit it together. Ask questions to help children explore their understanding of the story. For example, after reading "My Pet Mule" (page 35), ask:

- Who is this story about? (*a pet mule*)
- What is the mule's name? (*Luke*)
- What can this mule do? (*hum a tune, play the flute, use a computer*)
- Do you think this mule is real or make-believe? How do you know? (*make-believe; mules can't do those things*)

Teaching Tip

You can easily adapt any story to focus on new words. Simply fill in the original target words and create blanks to target a new set of words. Use liquid eraser to replace the words in the Word Bank with the new set of words. For example, you might adapt "Jen Helps Grandpa" (page 18) to provide practice with the sight words *the* and *you*. Follow the same procedure (filling in words and leaving blanks for the new target words) to create new pocket chart activities.

Fluency Practice

The brevity of the stories makes them just right for fluency practice.

1. Copy a story on chart paper. Have children help you fill in the missing words.

2. Read the story aloud, modeling good reading behaviors for pacing, expression, punctuation, and inflection. For example, use stories with more than one character (and dialogue) to model how to use a different voice for each character. Model how question marks and exclamation points give you clues about expression.

3. Read the story together, using an echo-reading approach. You read one line and children repeat it, echoing your pacing, phrasing, and intonation.

4. Read the story as a group, again encouraging children to follow along with pacing, phrasing, and intonation.

Story Switcheroo

Have some fun with the stories, using the characters, settings, and events to create new stories.

1. Write characters' names on slips of paper. Place them in a bag and label it "Characters." Do the same with story settings (such as "a bear's cave"), events (such as "camping"), and problems (such as "being homesick").

2. Let children take turns choosing a slip from each bag. Use the elements to tell a new story. Write it on chart paper and let children illustrate to create a new set of stories to read.

Answer Key

Page 15

Sad Bab!

Answers:
Bab, sad, ran, rag, nap, Dad, wag

Word Search Answers:

Page 20

Hit the Ball!

Answers:
Tim, hit, win, him, kid, did

Word Search Answers:

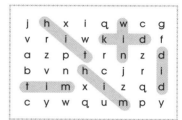

Page 16

Nan's Shopping Bag

Answers:
Nan, had, bag, jam, ham, pan, can

Word Search Answers:

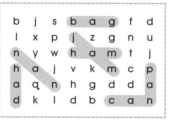

Page 21

Dot the Frog

Answers:
Dot, not, log, sob, dog, lot

Word Search Answers:

Page 17

Pep Goes to the Vet

Answers:
pet, Pep, ten, leg, vet, get

Word Search Answers:

Page 22

Corn on the Cob

Answers:
Bob, pot, top, hot, got, cob

Word Search Answers:

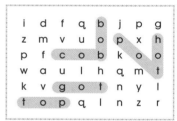

Page 18

Jen Helps Grandpa

Answers:
hen, fed, Jen, let, Yes, yet, wet

Word Search Answers:

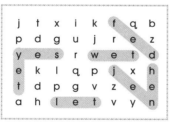

Page 23

A Bug on a Rug

Answers:
bug, Bud, rug, but, sun, hum

Word Search Answers:

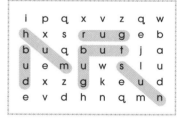

Page 19

Does It Fit?

Answers:
Min, zip, fit, big, fix, did

Word Search Answers:

Page 24

Little Cub

Answers:
cub, fun, hug, mud, dug, tub

Word Search Answers:

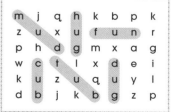

Page 25
Let's Trade!

Answers:
trade, Kate, gave,
skates, cape, made

Word Search Answers:

Page 30
Things I Like

Answers:
five, ride, slice,
write, hide, time

Word Search Answers:
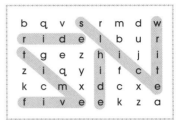

Page 26
Rainy Day

Answers:
paint, pail, gray,
rain, day, play

Word Search Answers:

Page 31
A Good Try!

Answers:
bright, high, by,
try, right, kind

Word Search Answers:
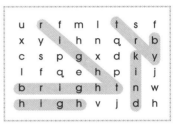

Page 27
What Did Jean See?

Answers:
Jean, tree, need, see,
eating, bees, sleep

Word Search Answers:
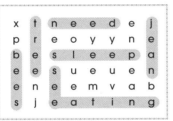

Page 32
A Note From Rose

Answers:
Rose, home, wrote,
phone, note, hope

Word Search Answers:

Page 28
A Horse Named Chief

Answers:
She, niece, me,
Chief, field, We

Word Search Answers:
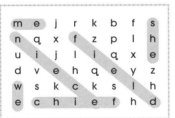

Page 33
A Toad on the Road

Answers:
road, toad, croaked,
So, Go, told, gold

Word Search Answers:
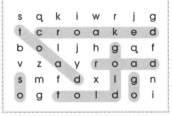

Page 29
A Messy Monkey

Answers:
monkey, messy, honey,
money, very, tidy

Word Search Answers:
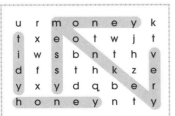

Page 34
Snowy Day

Answers:
Joe, snow, doe,
blow, know

Word Search Answers:
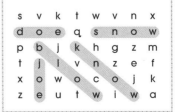

Answer Key

Page 35

My Pet Mule

Answers:
mule, Luke, tune,
flute, use

Word Search Answers:

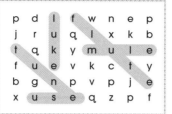

Page 40

A Deer Was Here!

Answers:
clear, near, deer,
Cheer, here

Word Search Answers:

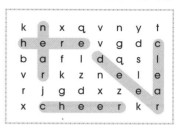

Page 36

Under the Stars

Answers:
Marta, yard, hard,
dark, stars, far

Word Search Answers:

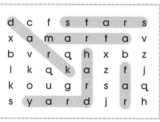

Page 41

Draw a Picture

Answers:
Paul, draw, taught,
always, dawn, all

Word Search Answers:

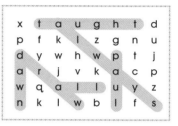

Page 37

Irma and the Bird

Answers:
girl, bird, hurt, her,
nurse, chirp

Word Search Answers:

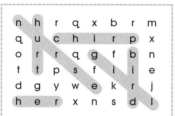

Page 42

A Noisy Pair

Answers:
Roy, voice, join,
enjoy, noisy

Word Search Answers:

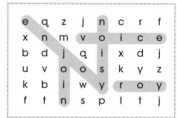

Page 38

A Good Sport

Answers:
sport, morning, forth,
score, for, more

Word Search Answers:

Page 43

Lost and Found

Answers:
brown, cow, out,
shouted, found, town

Word Search Answers:

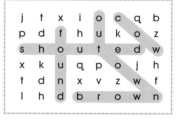

Page 39

A Bear and a Hare

Answers:
bear, hare, Where,
there, share, pair

Word Search Answers:

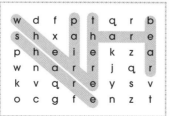

Page 44

A Blue Kite

Answers:
Sue, blue, knew,
flew, true

Word Search Answers:

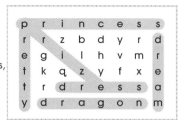

Page 45
A Pool Is Cool!

Answers:
too, pool, cool,
room, noon, Soon

Page 50
A Pretty Dream

Answers:
dream, princess, dress,
pretty, dragon, prize

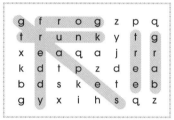

Page 46
A Good Time

Answers:
woods, brook, took,
stood, Look, good

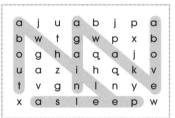

Page 51
Trudy and Freddy

Answers:
tree, frog, Freddy,
grapes, trunk, grab

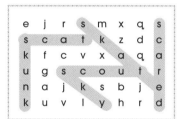

Page 47
Asleep and Awake

Answers:
asleep, above, again,
about, awhile, awake

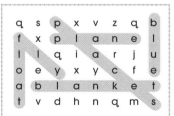

Page 52
Scat!

Answers:
sky, skate, Scout,
skunk, scared, Scat

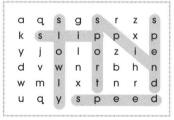

Page 48
Fly Away!
Answers:

plane, blanket, blue,
float, fly, places

Page 53
The Best Sport

Answers:
sport, spend, slowly,
speed, spin, slip

Word Search Answers:

Page 49
Silly Crow

Answers:
crow, creek, brag,
brave, cry, bring

Word Search Answers:

Page 54
Snug and Warm

Answers:
small, smile, snack,
smells, snow, snug

Answer Key

Page 55
Twinkle

Answers:
Twinkle, sweet, twenty, swim, starts, stand

Word Search Answers:

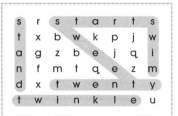

Page 56
An Old Quilt

Answers:
gift, quilt, child, lift, felt, cold

Word Search Answers:

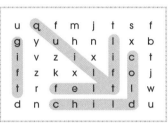

Page 57
A Band of Chimps

Answers:
chimps, and, band, went, jump, want

Word Search Answers:

Page 58
Hang On!

Answers:
Frank, sang, sink, long, hung, Thank

Word Search Answers:

Page 59
My Shadow

Answers:
thin, short, think, shake, thank, shows

Word Search Answers:

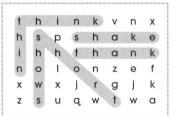

Page 60
Chase the Waves!

Answers:
Mitch, catch, chase, chooses, chip, watch

Word Search Answers:

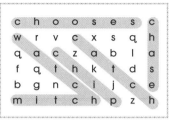

Page 61
Phil's Photos

Answers:
whale, Phil, photos, phone, Why, White

Word Search Answers:

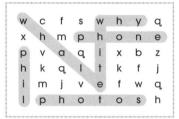

Page 62
Country Days

Answers:
days, buses, porches, chairs, lunches, frogs

Word Search Answers:

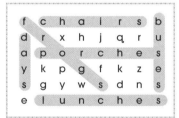

Page 63
It's Raining!

Answers:
playing, started, picked, looked, flying

Word Search Answers:

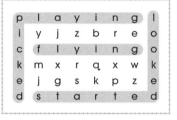

Page 64
We'll Find It!

Answers:
can't, don't, isn't, I'll, We'll

Word Search Answers:

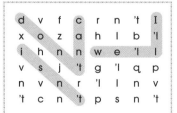

CVC Words With Short a

Look at the Word Bank.
Use the words to fill in the blanks.
Then read the story!

Word Bank

rag

wag

Bab

Dad

sad

ran

nap

Sad Bab!

_____ was a _____ pup.

She was home alone.

First, she _____ around the house.

Next, she played with a _____ doll.

Then Bab took a _____.

Soon Mom and _____ came home.

Look at Bab _____ her tail!

Look at the Word Bank.
Circle the words here.
Then read them!

k	n	m	q	v	b	a	b
x	a	w	t	s	g	d	s
b	p	i	a	h	a	a	b
h	v	k	z	g	c	d	u
r	a	g	d	c	c	y	l
x	s	r	a	n	f	e	u

CVC Words With Short a

Look at the Word Bank.
Use the words to fill in the blanks.
Then read the story!

Word Bank

can

Nan

pan

jam

ham

bag

had

Nan's Shopping Bag

_____ went shopping.

She _____ a big shopping _____.

Nan bought a jar of _____.

She bought a _____ for dinner.

Then she bought a pot and a _____.

"Now my bag is full," said Nan.

"I _____ go home!"

Word Search

Look at the Word Bank.
Circle the words here.
Then read them!

b	j	s	b	a	g	f	d
l	x	p	j	z	g	n	u
n	y	w	h	a	m	t	j
h	a	j	v	k	m	c	p
a	q	n	h	g	d	d	a
d	k	l	d	b	c	a	n

CVC Words With Short e

Look at the Word Bank.
Use the words to fill in the blanks.
Then read the story!

Word Bank

get

vet

pet

Pep

leg

ten

Pep Goes to the Vet

I have a _____ cat.

His name is _____.

He is more than _____ years old!

One day, Pep hurt his _____.

So Mom and I took him to the _____.

"Will Pep _____ better?" I asked.

"He will be just fine!" said the vet.

Look at the Word Bank.
Circle the words here.
Then read them!

p	q	z	j	l	c	r	f
x	e	m	t	e	n	h	s
b	p	p	q	g	x	d	j
u	v	q	l	g	k	y	l
k	e	u	w	z	e	f	y
f	t	k	s	p	e	t	l

CVC Words With Short e

Look at the Word Bank.
Use the words to fill in the blanks.
Then read the story!

Jen Helps Grandpa

Word Bank

wet

yet

let

fed

hen

Jen

yes

"Did you feed the _____?" asked Grandpa.

"I _____ the hen," said _____.

"Did you _____ the horses out?" asked Grandpa.

"_____, I did," said Jen.

"Did you water the plants _____?" asked

Grandpa.

"Yes, the plants are _____," said Jen.

"Then go and have fun!" said Grandpa.

Word Search

Look at the Word Bank.
Circle the words here.
Then read them!

j	t	x	i	k	f	q	b
p	d	g	u	j	r	e	z
y	e	s	r	w	e	t	d
e	k	l	q	p	j	x	h
t	d	p	g	v	z	e	e
a	h	l	e	t	v	y	n

CVC Words With Short *i*

Look at the Word Bank.
Use the words to fill in the blanks.
Then read the story!

Does It Fit?

Word Bank

fix

fit

did

Min

zip

big

_____ put on her jacket.

She could not _____ it up!

"My jacket does not _____," said Min.

"It is not _____ enough," said Mom.

"Can you _____ it?" asked Min.

Mom _____ not think so.

"We will get you a new jacket!" said Mom.

Look at the Word Bank.
Circle the words here.
Then read them!

j	w	x	u	i	l	g	m
b	r	f	i	x	k	u	a
i	z	y	i	r	z	k	z
g	p	q	x	t	b	i	h
z	d	i	d	c	w	y	p
c	h	t	m	i	n	x	f

CVC Words With Short *i*

Look at the Word Bank.
Use the words to fill in the blanks.
Then read the story!

Hit the Ball!

Word Bank

kid

did

Tim

him

hit

win

_____ is up at bat.

"I hope I can _____ the ball," he said.

"I want my team to _____."

Now the ball was coming at _____.

Tim hit the ball and ran.

"Look at that _____ go!" yelled the crowd.

Tim _____ it! He made a home run!

Look at the Word Bank.
Circle the words here.
Then read them!

j	h	x	i	q	w	c	g
v	r	i	w	k	i	d	f
a	z	p	t	r	n	z	d
b	v	n	h	c	j	r	i
t	i	m	x	i	z	q	d
c	y	w	q	u	m	p	y

CVC Words With Short *o*

Look at the Word Bank.
Use the words to fill in the blanks.
Then read the story!

Dot the Frog

Once there was a frog named _____.

She was very sad.

"I do _____ have a friend," she said.

Dot sat on a _____ and began

to _____.

Just then, a _____ came by.

"I will be your friend," said the dog.

"We will have a _____ of fun!"

Word Bank

dog

log

sob

Dot

lot

not

Word Search

Look at the Word Bank.
Circle the words here.
Then read them!

s	g	x	p	b	n	h	p
j	d	z	n	j	o	u	w
t	q	o	m	d	t	k	l
v	l	u	t	r	q	c	o
k	x	o	w	l	n	y	t
w	d	o	g	b	s	o	b

Name _____   Date _____

Look at the Word Bank.
Use the words to fill in the blanks.
Then read the story!

Word Bank

got

pot

hot

Bob

cob

top

Corn on the Cob

_____ was making dinner.

First, he put water in the _____.

Then he put the pot on _____ of the stove.

Soon the water was _____.

Bob _____ the corn and put it in the pot.

What did Bob eat? Corn on the _____!

Look at the Word Bank.
Circle the words here.
Then read them!

i	d	f	q	b	j	p	g
z	m	v	u	o	p	x	h
p	f	c	o	b	k	o	o
w	a	u	l	h	q	m	t
k	v	g	o	t	n	y	l
t	o	p	q	l	n	z	r

CVC Words With Short *u*

Look at the Word Bank.
Use the words to fill in the blanks.
Then read the story!

Word Bank

sun

rug

bug

but

Bud

hum

A Bug on a Rug

Once there was a little _____ named

_____.

Bud lived on a _____ inside a house.

It was a nice home, _____ Bud was not happy.

He wanted to be outside in the _____.

One day, Bud left the rug. Now he lives outside.

You can hear Bud _____ all day long!

Look at the Word Bank.
Circle the words here.
Then read them!

i	p	q	x	v	z	q	w
h	x	s	r	u	g	e	b
b	u	q	b	u	t	j	a
u	e	m	u	w	s	l	u
d	x	z	g	k	e	u	d
e	v	d	h	n	q	m	n

CVC Words With Short *u*

Look at the Word Bank.
Use the words to fill in the blanks.
Then read the story!

Little Cub

A little _____ went out to play.

"Have _____!" said Mom.

She gave him a _____.

The little cub played in the _____ all day.

He _____ a deep hole and made mud pies.

When the little cub came home, Mom said,

"Get into the _____ and take a bath!"

Word Bank

dug

hug

fun

cub

tub

mud

Word Search

Look at the Word Bank.
Circle the words here.
Then read them!

m	j	q	h	k	b	p	k
z	u	x	u	f	u	n	r
p	h	d	g	m	x	a	g
w	c	t	l	x	d	e	i
k	u	z	u	q	u	y	l
d	b	j	k	b	g	z	p

Words With Long *a: a-e*

Look at the Word Bank.
Use the words to fill in the blanks.
Then read the story!

Word Bank

gave
cape
made
Kate
skates
trade

Let's Trade!

It's fun to _____ things.

My friend _____ and I trade all the time.

Last week, I _____ Kate a pair

of _____.

She gave me a pretty _____.

That trade _____ us both very happy!

Word Search

Look at the Word Bank.
Circle the words here.
Then read them!

m	d	t	s	x	z	p	q
e	a	z	r	t	y	g	b
u	c	d	y	a	j	a	l
k	a	t	e	z	d	v	n
b	p	s	k	a	t	e	s
c	e	x	q	g	e	x	f

Words With Long *a*: *ai, ay*

Look at the Word Bank.
Use the words to fill in the blanks.
Then read the story!

Word Bank

day

play

gray

rain

pail

paint

Rainy Day

Grandma and I will _____ the porch.

We have our brushes.

We have a _____ of

_____ paint.

Then it starts to _____!

"Tomorrow is another _____,"

says Grandma.

"Let's go inside and _____."

Look at the Word Bank.
Circle the words here.
Then read them!

g	p	a	i	l	d	x	y
l	r	a	u	n	a	d	j
u	g	q	i	x	y	p	l
f	t	w	z	n	k	l	f
r	a	i	n	d	t	a	p
d	f	b	g	r	a	y	f

Words With Long *e*: *ea*, *ee*

Look at the Word Bank.
Use the words to fill in the blanks.
Then read the story!

Word Bank

bees

eating

Jean

need

see

sleep

tree

What Did Jean See?

_____ sat under a big _____.

"I _____ a nap," she said.

But there were so many things to _____!

Jean looked at some ducks _____ grass.

Then she looked at some _____ buzzing

around flowers. "I will _____ later,"

Jean said. "I'd rather look around!"

Word Search

Look at the Word Bank.
Circle the words here.
Then read them!

x	t	n	e	e	d	e	j
p	r	e	o	y	y	n	e
b	e	s	l	e	e	p	a
e	e	s	u	e	u	e	n
e	n	e	e	m	v	a	b
s	j	e	a	t	i	n	g

Words With Long *e*: *e, ie*

Look at the Word Bank.
Use the words to fill in the blanks.
Then read the story!

Word Bank

me

she

we

Chief

field

niece

A Horse Named Chief

Aunt Lana is my favorite aunt.

_____ lives on a horse ranch.

I'm glad that I'm her _____!

She lets _____ ride a horse

named _____.

I ride Chief around the _____.

_____ make such a good team!

Look at the Word Bank.
Circle the words here.
Then read them!

m	e	j	r	k	b	f	s
n	q	x	f	z	p	l	h
u	i	j	l	i	q	x	e
d	v	e	h	q	e	y	z
w	s	k	c	k	s	l	h
e	c	h	i	e	f	h	d

Words With Long e: ey, y

Look at the Word Bank.
Use the words to fill in the blanks.
Then read the story!

Word Bank

money

honey

monkey

tidy

very

messy

A Messy Monkey

Perry was a lazy _____.

His house was _____ and sloppy!

One day, Perry wanted to buy some bread

and _____.

He looked all over for his _____.

But he couldn't find it. So Perry cleaned his house.

Now his house is _____ _____!

Word Search

Look at the Word Bank.
Circle the words here.
Then read them!

```
u  r  m  o  n  e  y  k
t  x  e  o  t  w  j  t
i  w  s  b  n  t  h  v
d  f  s  t  h  k  z  e
y  x  y  d  q  b  e  r
h  o  n  e  y  n  t  y
```

Words With Long *i*: *i-e*

Look at the Word Bank.
Use the words to fill in the blanks.
Then read the story!

Word Bank
hide
ride
five
write
time
slice

Things I Like

Here are _____ things that I like.

I like to _____ my bike.

I like to eat a _____ of pizza.

I like to _____ my name.

I like to play _____-and-seek.

I like to have a good _____ with

people I like!

Word Search

Look at the Word Bank.
Circle the words here.
Then read them!

b	q	v	s	r	m	d	w
r	i	d	e	l	b	u	r
t	g	e	z	h	i	j	i
z	i	q	y	i	f	c	t
k	c	m	x	d	c	x	e
f	i	v	e	e	k	z	a

Words With Long *i*: *i, igh, y*

Look at the Word Bank.
Use the words to fill in the blanks.
Then read the story!

Word Bank

kind

right

bright

high

by

try

A Good Try!

One _____ morning, Rabbit saw a peach tree.

He wanted a peach, but they were too

_____ up.

Just then, Squirrel came _____.

"I'll _____ to get one for you," she said.

So she ran _____ up to the top and picked one!

"You are very _____!" said Rabbit.

"Let's share it."

Word Search

Look at the Word Bank.
Circle the words here.
Then read them!

u	r	f	m	l	t	s	f
x	y	i	h	n	q	r	b
c	s	p	g	x	d	k	y
l	f	q	e	h	p	i	j
b	r	i	g	h	t	n	w
h	i	g	h	v	j	d	h

Words With Long *o*: *o-e*

Look at the Word Bank.
Use the words to fill in the blanks.
Then read the story!

Word Bank

phone

note

home

hope

Rose

wrote

A Note From Rose

_____ went away to camp.

At first, she missed her _____.

She _____ many letters to Mom and Dad.

She also called them on the _____.

Then Rose wasn't homesick anymore!

This is the _____ she wrote: "I'm having fun.

I _____ you don't miss me too much!"

Look at the Word Bank.
Circle the words here.
Then read them!

z	h	p	q	d	x	h	m
y	o	z	h	q	g	u	h
r	m	b	q	o	b	k	o
o	e	v	d	k	n	q	p
s	z	w	r	o	t	e	e
e	n	o	t	e	a	w	c

Words With Long _o_: _o_, _oa_

Look at the Word Bank.
Use the words to fill in the blanks.
Then read the story!

A Toad on the Road

Word Bank

go

so

told

gold

croaked

toad

road

A man was walking along a _____.

Then he met a little _____.

"I'm hungry," _____ the toad.

_____ the man gave him some food.

"_____ home now," croaked the toad.

So the man did as he was _____.

In his house, there was a pot of _____!

Look at the Word Bank.
Circle the words here.
Then read them!

s	q	k	i	w	r	j	g
t	c	r	o	a	k	e	d
b	o	l	j	h	g	q	f
v	z	a	y	r	o	a	d
s	m	f	d	x	l	g	n
o	g	t	o	l	d	o	i

Words With Long *o*: *oe*, *ow*

Look at the Word Bank.
Use the words to fill in the blanks.
Then read the story!

Word Bank

doe

Joe

blow

know

snow

Snowy Day

_____ looked out the window.

The _____ was falling.

He saw a _____ run by.

He heard the wind _____.

"I _____ the snow won't last," said Joe.

"I have to go out and make a snowman!"

Word Search

Look at the Word Bank.
Circle the words here.
Then read them!

s	v	k	t	w	v	n	x
d	o	e	q	s	n	o	w
p	b	j	k	h	g	z	m
t	j	l	v	n	z	e	f
x	o	w	o	c	o	j	k
z	e	u	t	w	i	w	a

Words With Long *u*: *u-e*

Look at the Word Bank.
Use the words to fill in the blanks.
Then read the story!

Word Bank
flute
mule
Luke
tune
use

My Pet Mule

I have a pet _____ named _____.

He has many special talents.

Luke can hum a _____.

He can play the _____.

He even knows how to _____ a computer.

What an amazing and amusing mule!

Look at the Word Bank.
Circle the words here.
Then read them!

p	d	l	f	w	n	e	p
j	r	u	q	l	x	k	b
t	q	k	y	m	u	l	e
f	u	e	v	k	c	t	y
b	g	n	p	v	p	j	e
x	u	s	e	q	z	p	f

Words With the /är/ Sound: *ar*

Look at the Word Bank.
Use the words to fill in the blanks.
Then read the story!

Word Bank

dark

far

hard

Marta

stars

yard

Under the Stars

_____ and Grandma were camping out

in their _____.

The ground felt _____, but Marta didn't mind.

It was very _____ inside the tent.

So Marta peeked outside.

She looked up at the moon and _____.

They didn't seem _____ away at all.

Look at the Word Bank.
Circle the words here.
Then read them!

d	c	f	s	t	a	r	s
x	a	m	a	r	t	a	v
b	v	r	q	h	x	b	z
l	k	q	k	a	z	f	j
k	o	u	g	r	s	a	q
s	y	a	r	d	j	r	h

Words With the /ûr/ Sound: *er, ir, ur*

Look at the Word Bank.
Use the words to fill in the blanks.
Then read the story!

Irma and the Bird

Word Bank

her

bird

chirp

girl

hurt

nurse

A _____ named Irma was picking flowers.

She saw a little _____ on the ground.

The bird's wing was _____.

So Irma took him to _____ home.

"I will _____ you until you are well,"

she said to the bird.

Soon the bird began to _____ again!

Word Search

Look at the Word Bank.
Circle the words here.
Then read them!

n	h	r	q	x	b	r	m
q	u	c	h	i	r	p	x
o	r	r	q	g	f	b	n
t	t	p	s	f	i	i	e
d	g	y	w	e	k	r	j
h	e	r	x	n	s	d	l

Words With the /ôr/ Sound: *or, ore*

Look at the Word Bank.
Use the words to fill in the blanks.
Then read the story!

Word Bank

for

forth

more

score

morning

sport

A Good Sport

Corey's favorite _____ was soccer.

One _____, Corey was in a soccer game.

He ran back and _____ on the field.

Soon the _____ was tied.

Then Corey made a goal _____ his team.

"What can be _____ fun than that?"

he asked.

Word Search

Look at the Word Bank.
Circle the words here.
Then read them!

x	e	v	z	b	q	n	x
f	y	s	c	o	r	e	j
o	m	p	d	q	x	p	m
r	m	o	r	n	i	n	g
t	h	r	r	k	p	z	a
h	s	t	l	e	f	o	r

Words With the /âr/ Sound: *air, are, ear, ere*

Look at the Word Bank.
Use the words to fill in the blanks.
Then read the story!

Word Bank

pair

hare

share

bear

there

where

A Bear and a Hare

A _____ was sleeping in her cave.

Suddenly, a little _____ ran in!

"_____ are you going?" asked the bear.

"It's so cold out _____!" said the hare.

"Will you _____ your home with me?"

"You can stay," said the bear.

Now the _____ are best friends!

Look at the Word Bank.
Circle the words here.
Then read them!

w	d	f	p	t	q	r	b
s	h	x	a	h	a	r	e
p	h	e	i	e	k	z	a
w	n	a	r	r	j	q	r
k	v	q	r	e	y	s	v
o	c	g	f	e	n	z	t

Words With the /îr/ Sound: *ear, eer, ere*

Look at the Word Bank.
Use the words to fill in the blanks.
Then read the story!

A Deer Was Here!

Word Bank

here

cheer

deer

near

clear

It was a _____, sunny day.

But I was sad because summer was ending.

I sat on a big rock _____ the lake.

Then guess what happened!

A _____ came over to me.

"_____ up!" she said. "It's so

pretty _____!"

Then she ran off, and I felt happy again.

Word Search

Look at the Word Bank.
Circle the words here.
Then read them!

k	n	x	q	v	n	y	t
h	e	r	e	v	g	d	c
b	a	f	l	d	q	s	l
v	r	k	z	n	e	l	e
r	j	g	d	x	z	e	a
x	c	h	e	e	r	k	r

Fill-in-the-Blank Stories: Phonics © 2008 by Linda B. Ross. Scholastic Teaching Resources.

Name _____ Date _____

Words With the /ô/ Sound: *a, au, aw*

Look at the Word Bank.
Use the words to fill in the blanks.
Then read the story!

Word Bank

all

always

dawn

draw

Paul

taught

Draw a Picture

_____ is an artist.

He likes to _____ and paint.

No one _____ him how.

He was _____ good at it.

Once he got up at _____ to paint

the sunrise!

I like that picture best of _____.

Word Search

Look at the Word Bank.
Circle the words here.
Then read them!

x	t	a	u	g	h	t	d
p	f	k	l	z	g	n	u
d	y	w	h	w	p	t	j
a	r	j	v	k	a	c	p
w	q	a	l	l	u	y	z
n	k	l	w	b	l	f	s

Words With the /oi/ Sound: oi, oy

Look at the Word Bank.
Use the words to fill in the blanks.
Then read the story!

Word Bank

join

noisy

voice

Roy

enjoy

A Noisy Pair

_____ likes to sing.

He has a good _____.

When Roy sings, his dog, Floyd, likes to

_____ in.

Roy and Floyd _____ singing together.

"We are a _____ pair!" says Roy.

Word Search

Look at the Word Bank.
Circle the words here.
Then read them!

e	q	z	j	n	c	r	f
x	n	m	v	o	i	c	e
b	d	j	q	i	x	d	j
u	v	o	o	s	k	y	z
k	b	i	w	y	r	o	y
f	t	n	s	p	l	t	j

Words With the /ou/ Sound: *ou, ow*

Look at the Word Bank.
Use the words to fill in the blanks.
Then read the story!

Word Bank
found
out
shouted
brown
cow
town

Lost and Found

I have a _____ and white

_____ named Flower.

One day she went _____ for a walk

and didn't come home.

"Where are you, Flower?" I _____.

At last, I _____ her.

She was on the other side of _____!

Word Search

Look at the Word Bank.
Circle the words here.
Then read them!

j	t	x	i	o	c	q	b
p	d	f	h	u	k	o	z
s	h	o	u	t	e	d	w
x	k	u	q	p	o	j	h
t	d	n	x	v	z	w	f
l	h	d	b	r	o	w	n

Words With the /ü/ Sound: *ew, ue*

Look at the Word Bank.
Use the words to fill in the blanks.
Then read the story!

Word Bank

flew

knew

blue

Sue

true

A Blue Kite

A girl named _____ had a

_____ kite.

One windy day, the kite blew away!

Sue was sad. She _____ her kite was gone.

The next day, a bird _____ into her yard.

It had the blue kite in its beak!

Do you think this story is _____?

Word Search

Look at the Word Bank.
Circle the words here.
Then read them!

j	w	x	u	i	p	g	z
s	r	t	z	b	l	u	e
u	z	y	r	s	k	w	q
e	n	q	x	u	n	m	h
z	v	w	k	c	e	q	p
c	h	f	l	e	w	x	f

Fill-in-the-Blank Stories: Phonics © 2008 by Linda B. Ross. Scholastic Teaching Resources.

Name _____ Date _____

Words With the /ü/ Sound: *oo*

Look at the Word Bank.
Use the words to fill in the blanks.
Then read the story!

Word Bank

noon

soon

cool

pool

too

room

A Pool Is Cool!

It's _____ hot to play outside.

So Ricky and I go to the town _____.

It's the best place to _____ off!

There is lots of _____ to swim and dive.

At _____, we stop and eat lunch.

Then we rest for a while.

_____ we'll jump back in!

Look at the Word Bank.
Circle the words here.
Then read them!

j	c	x	i	p	t	c	g
v	y	o	w	o	s	o	j
s	z	x	o	o	k	z	o
o	v	n	h	l	j	r	u
o	b	m	x	r	o	o	m
n	o	o	n	q	m	p	d

Words With the /ŭ/ Sound: oo

Look at the Word Bank.
Use the words to fill in the blanks.
Then read the story!

Word Bank

good

stood

brook

look

took

woods

A Good Time

Dad and I walked in the _____.

We stopped at a pretty _____.

We _____ off our shoes and socks.

Then we _____ in the cool water.

"_____ at the little fish swimming

around our feet!" I said.

We had a _____ time!

Word Search

Look at the Word Bank.
Circle the words here.
Then read them!

g	k	x	w	b	n	h	p
j	o	z	o	j	x	b	w
l	u	o	o	m	v	r	l
v	o	u	d	r	q	o	v
k	x	o	s	t	o	o	d
t	o	o	k	b	s	k	z

Fill-in-the-Blank Stories: Phonics © 2008 by Linda B. Ross. Scholastic Teaching Resources.

Words With the /ə/ Sound: a

Look at the Word Bank.
Use the words to fill in the blanks.
Then read the story!

Asleep and Awake

Word Bank
about
above
again
asleep
awake
awhile

Before I fall _____, this is what I do.

I look at the moon and stars high _____.

I read my favorite book _____.

Then I shut off the light and think _____ tomorrow.

After _____, I stop thinking.

The next thing I know it's morning, and I'm

wide _____!

Look at the Word Bank.
Circle the words here.
Then read them!

a	j	u	a	b	j	p	a
b	w	t	g	w	p	x	b
o	g	h	a	q	a	j	o
u	a	z	i	h	q	k	v
t	v	g	n	l	n	y	e
x	a	s	l	e	e	p	w

Name _____   Date _____

Words With *bl, fl, pl*

Look at the Word Bank.
Use the words to fill in the blanks.
Then read the story!

Word Bank

blanket

blue

float

fly

places

plane

Fly Away!

I was on a _____ for the first time.

We were going to Florida to visit Grandma.

I got a pillow and a _____.

I looked out the window at the _____ sky.

I saw fluffy clouds _____ by.

It's fun to _____ to new _____!

Word Search

Look at the Word Bank.
Circle the words here.
Then read them!

q	s	p	x	v	z	q	b
f	x	p	l	a	n	e	l
l	l	q	i	a	r	j	u
o	e	y	x	y	c	f	e
a	b	l	a	n	k	e	t
t	v	d	h	n	q	m	s

Words With *br, cr*

Look at the Word Bank.
Use the words to fill in the blanks.
Then read the story!

Word Bank

brag

brave

bring

creek

crow

cry

Silly Crow

A silly _____ lived near a _____.

He liked to _____ about how great he was.

"I'm so smart and _____!" he said.

Soon the other birds left him alone.

The crow felt sad and started to _____.

"I'll stop bragging," he said.

"That will _____ my friends back."

And it did!

Look at the Word Bank.
Circle the words here.
Then read them!

d	b	q	h	b	j	p	k
c	r	o	w	r	r	n	f
p	i	m	q	a	x	a	v
c	n	t	l	v	f	j	g
r	g	c	r	e	e	k	l
y	x	j	k	w	q	z	p

Words With *dr, pr*

Look at the Word Bank.
Use the words to fill in the blanks.
Then read the story!

Word Bank

dragon

dream

dress

pretty

princess

prize

A Pretty Dream

Last night, I went to sleep and had a _____.

I lived in a castle, and I was a _____.

I wore a long _____ and

a _____ crown.

I had a pet _____ named Drake.

We were in a race and won first _____.

I was so proud!

Word Search

Look at the Word Bank.
Circle the words here.
Then read them!

p	r	i	n	c	e	s	s
r	r	z	b	d	y	r	d
e	g	i	l	h	v	m	r
t	k	q	z	y	f	x	e
t	r	d	r	e	s	s	a
y	d	r	a	g	o	n	m

Fill-in-the-Blank Stories: Phonics © 2008 by Linda B. Ross. Scholastic Teaching Resources.

Name _____ Date _____

Look at the Word Bank.
Use the words to fill in the blanks.
Then read the story!

Word Bank

Freddy

frog

grab

grapes

tree

trunk

Trudy and Freddy

Trudy the elephant sat under a _____.

Suddenly, a _____ fell right on Trudy's head!

"I'm sorry," said _____ the frog.

"I was reaching for the _____."

"No problem!" said Trudy.

"I'll use my _____ to _____ them."

And that's what she did!

Look at the Word Bank.
Circle the words here.
Then read them!

g	f	r	o	g	z	p	q
t	r	u	n	k	y	t	g
x	e	a	q	a	j	r	r
k	d	t	p	z	d	e	a
b	d	s	k	e	t	e	b
g	y	x	i	h	s	q	z

Words With *sc, sk*

Look at the Word Bank.
Use the words to fill in the blanks.
Then read the story!

Word Bank

scared

scat

Scout

skate

skunk

sky

Scat!

The sun is out, and the _____ is blue.

It is a great day to _____.

My dog, _____, is with me.

We are having fun. Then Scout sees

a _____!

He is _____, but I'm not.

"_____!" I say, and the skunk runs away.

Word Search

Look at the Word Bank.
Circle the words here.
Then read them!

e	j	r	s	m	x	q	s
s	c	a	t	k	z	d	c
k	f	c	v	x	a	q	a
u	g	s	c	o	u	t	r
n	a	j	k	s	b	j	e
k	u	v	l	y	h	r	d

Name _____   Date _____

Words With *sl, sp*

Look at the Word Bank.
Use the words to fill in the blanks.
Then read the story!

Word Bank
slip
slowly
speed
spend
spin
sport

The Best Sport

Ice skating is the best _____.

I _____ many hours on the ice.

At first, I skated very _____, but now

I skate with _____.

Last week, I learned how to _____ like a top!

Sometimes I _____ and fall, but I get

right back up. Watch me go!

Word Search

Look at the Word Bank.
Circle the words here.
Then read them!

a	q	s	g	s	r	z	s
k	s	l	i	p	p	x	p
y	j	o	l	o	z	i	e
d	v	w	n	r	b	h	n
w	m	l	x	t	n	r	d
u	q	y	s	p	e	e	d

Name _____   Date _____

Look at the Word Bank.
Use the words to fill in the blanks.
Then read the story!

Word Bank

smells

smile

small

snack

snow

snug

Snug and Warm

I make a snowman and give him two

_____ eyes, a long nose, and a

big _____.

Then I get hungry. So I go inside for a _____.

The soup _____ good and tastes even better!

I look out. It's starting to _____ again.

I feel _____ and warm inside.

Word Search

Look at the Word Bank.
Circle the words here.
Then read them!

g	s	n	u	g	d	x	y
l	r	m	u	n	s	d	j
u	g	q	e	x	m	p	s
f	t	w	z	l	i	l	n
s	n	a	c	k	l	x	o
s	m	a	l	l	e	s	w

Name _____ Date _____

Words With *st, sw, tw*

Look at the Word Bank.
Use the words to fill in the blanks.
Then read the story!

Word Bank

stand

starts

sweet

swim

Twinkle

twenty

Twinkle

A bird named _____ lives by a lake.

She has a _____ voice and knows

more than _____ songs!

Twinkle likes to watch people _____.

Swimmers like to hear Twinkle sing.

When she _____ singing,

swimmers _____ and clap.

Word Search

Look at the Word Bank.
Circle the words here.
Then read them!

s	r	s	t	a	r	t	s
t	x	b	w	k	p	j	w
a	g	z	b	e	j	q	i
n	f	m	t	q	e	z	m
d	x	t	w	e	n	t	y
t	w	i	n	k	l	e	u

Words With *ft, ld, lt*

Look at the Word Bank.
Use the words to fill in the blanks.
Then read the story!

Word Bank

gift

lift

child

cold

felt

quilt

An Old Quilt

Grandma gave me a birthday _____.

It was an old _____.

Grandma had it since she was a _____.

It was so heavy that I could hardly _____ it!

It _____ nice and soft.

It will keep me warm on _____ nights.

Word Search

Look at the Word Bank.
Circle the words here.
Then read them!

u	q	f	m	j	t	s	f
g	y	u	h	n	l	x	b
i	v	z	i	x	i	c	t
f	z	k	x	l	f	o	j
t	r	f	e	l	t	l	w
d	n	c	h	i	l	d	u

Name _____   Date _____

Look at the Word Bank.
Use the words to fill in the blanks.
Then read the story!

A Band of Chimps

Word Bank

and

band

chimps

jump

want

went

Once there were six _____.

They liked to sing _____ dance.

So the chimps formed a _____.

They _____ from town to town.

Many people came to see them.

They would _____ and cheer for

the chimps.

Now the chimps _____ to be on TV!

Look at the Word Bank.
Circle the words here.
Then read them!

z	w	e	n	t	x	c	m
y	q	s	j	l	g	h	u
r	w	b	k	u	r	i	q
x	k	a	q	v	m	m	y
s	z	n	n	c	d	p	h
a	n	d	k	t	r	s	j

Words With **ng, nk**

Look at the Word Bank.
Use the words to fill in the blanks.
Then read the story!

Word Bank

hung

long

sang

Frank

sink

thank

Hang On!

_____ and Fritz went out in a rowboat.

They _____ songs as they rowed.

They were having a good time.

Then the boat started to _____!

They were a _____ way from shore.

Frank and Fritz _____ on till help came.

"_____ you so much!" they said.

Word Search

Look at the Word Bank.
Circle the words here.
Then read them!

u	q	k	b	w	r	j	g
l	m	r	t	p	f	l	d
h	o	l	j	h	r	h	f
b	z	n	y	k	a	u	d
s	a	n	g	x	n	n	w
e	g	s	i	n	k	g	k

Name _____   Date _____

Words With *sh, th*

Look at the Word Bank.
Use the words to fill in the blanks.
Then read the story!

My Shadow

I like to watch my shadow.

Sometimes it is long and _____.

Sometimes it is _____ and wide.

I _____ my shadow has a good time.

When I dance and _____,

it does the same.

I should say "_____ you" to my shadow.

It _____ me how much fun I have!

Word Bank

shake

short

shows

thank

thin

think

Word Search

Look at the Word Bank.
Circle the words here.
Then read them!

t	h	i	n	k	v	n	x
h	s	p	s	h	a	k	e
i	h	h	t	h	a	n	k
n	o	l	o	n	z	e	f
x	w	x	j	r	g	j	k
z	s	u	q	w	t	w	a

Name _____ Date _____

Look at the Word Bank.
Use the words to fill in the blanks.
Then read the story!

Chase the Waves!

Word Bank
chase
chip
chooses
catch
Mitch
watch

Each summer, _____ visits his

cousin Charlie.

They play _____ at the beach.

They run in the ocean and _____ the waves!

In the afternoon, they buy ice cream cones.

Mitch always _____ vanilla.

Charlie always chooses chocolate _____.

Then they relax and _____ the ocean.

Look at the Word Bank.
Circle the words here.
Then read them!

c	h	o	o	s	e	s	c
w	r	v	c	x	s	q	h
q	a	c	z	a	b	l	a
f	q	t	h	k	t	d	s
b	g	n	c	i	j	c	e
m	i	t	c	h	p	z	h

Name _____   Date _____

Look at the Word Bank.
Use the words to fill in the blanks.
Then read the story!

Phil's Photos

Word Bank

Phil
phone
photos
whale
White
why

Once there was a _____

named _____.

He took great _____ and became famous.

One day, he got a _____ call from the President!

"_____ are you calling me?" asked Phil.

"I want to hang your photos in the _____

House," said the President.

"What an honor!" said Phil.

Look at the Word Bank.
Circle the words here.
Then read them!

w	c	f	s	w	h	y	q
x	h	m	p	h	o	n	e
p	v	a	q	i	x	b	z
h	k	q	l	t	k	f	j
i	m	j	v	e	f	w	q
l	p	h	o	t	o	s	h

Plurals -s and -es

Look at the Word Bank.
Use the words to fill in the blanks.
Then read the story!

Country Days

Word Bank

chairs

days

frogs

buses

lunches

porches

Aunt Carmen lives in the country.

Each summer, I spend ten _____ with her.

It's a quiet place. There are no trains

or _____.

Aunt Carmen's house has two _____.

The front porch has two comfortable _____.

We bring our _____ out there.

We watch the _____ jump in the grass.

Word Search

Look at the Word Bank.
Circle the words here.
Then read them!

f	c	h	a	i	r	s	b
d	r	x	h	j	q	r	u
a	p	o	r	c	h	e	s
y	k	p	g	f	k	z	e
s	g	y	w	s	d	n	s
e	l	u	n	c	h	e	s

Words With -ed and -ing

Look at the Word Bank.
Use the words to fill in the blanks.
Then read the story!

Word Bank

looked

picked

started

flying

playing

It's Raining!

Leo and I were _____ a game outside.

Then it _____ to rain.

We _____ up our game and ran inside.

Then we _____ out the window.

Birds were _____ to their nests.

They wanted to stay dry, too!

Word Search

Look at the Word Bank.
Circle the words here.
Then read them!

p	l	a	y	i	n	g	l
i	y	j	z	b	r	e	o
c	f	l	y	i	n	g	o
k	m	x	r	q	x	w	k
e	j	g	s	k	p	z	e
d	s	t	a	r	t	e	d

Name _____ Date _____

Contractions 'll and n't

Look at the Word Bank.
Use the words to fill in the blanks.
Then read the story!

Word Bank

we'll

I'll

isn't

don't

can't

We'll Find It!

My sneaker is missing, and I _____

find it!

I _____ know where I put it.

It _____ under my bed.

So _____ look in my closet.

It isn't in my closet. So I ask Mom for help.

"_____ look for it together!" she says.

Word Search

Look at the Word Bank.
Circle the words here.
Then read them!

d	v	f	c	r	n	't	I
x	o	z	a	h	l	b	'l
i	h	n	n	w	e	'l	l
v	s	j	't	g	'l	q	p
n	v	n	r	'l	l	n	v
't	c	n	't	p	s	n	't

Fill-in-the-Blank Stories: Phonics © 2008 by Linda B. Ross. Scholastic Teaching Resources.